Odes for the Soul… Poetry That Heals

Volume 2: Blue Flames from the Cocoon

J.R. Jones

Odes for the Soul... Poetry That Heals: Volume 2: Blue Flames from the Cocoon

Copyright © 2012 by J.R. Jones

All rights reserved solely by the author. No part of this book may be reproduced or transmitted in any form or by any means without written permission of the author.

ISBN : 978-0615704869

Dedication

I dedicate this book to the flames in my life: my mother, my grandmother, my sister, aunts, and a bouquet of family and friends, who have inspired my poetry. Thanks women for giving me a complex mix of creative fire to generate the blue flame that I am today. I'm ready to spread more fire.

Table of Contents

A Dream in Black and White	~	6
Afro Chick in a Spring Love Mist	~	7
Angel Wings of Prayer	~	8
Beautifully Black	~	9
Beholding Beauty in Simple Things	~	10
Birth of a Mommy	~	11
Blue Skies into Rain	~	12
Boxed In	~	13
Capital Puppets	~	14
Chocolate Fervor	~	15
Confessions of a Hypocrite	~	16
Dirty Talk	~	17
(Easy) This Friday	~	18
Explain This	~	19
First Date (Cold)	~	20
First Date (Warm)	~	21
For a Black Cause (Bettin on Black)	~	22
Groove Rainbows	~	23
I Need To Be in Love with a Taurus	~	24
In Love Behind the Scenes	~	25
Jazzy Mistletoe	~	26
Just Take Me	~	27
Love Letter to a Fiancé	~	28
Love Song of Jacinta	~	29
Make Love Simple	~	30
Midnight Stand	~	31
On a Summer's Day (Maybe on a Friday)	~	32
Peanut Butter Speaks	~	33

Photographing Beauty	~	34
Please Believe Me	~	35
Poppa Holiday (Holiday Poppa)	~	36
Powerful Hero	~	37
Power Running Things	~	38
Serendipity	~	39
Spicy Fight	~	40
Sunday Daze	~	41
Surviving Jasmine	~	42
The Year for Release of Minor Things~		43
Unthankful	~	44
(Young Love Rebel) Rebel Seventeen at Hamburger King	~	45

A Dream in Black and White

If it were simple/like Black and White.
Blue eyes looking/into brown eyes,
And seeing reflections/of themselves.
If it were only simple/like Black and White.
Black skin would flow easily/against white skin,
The contrast would be obvious/oblivious.
The grey areas/would not exist.
Life lived would be/harmonious bliss.

No socioeconomic lists/
No bourgeois classes/
No ghetto baby mommas/
No absent baby daddies.

Just suburbia/moms and dads.
Brothers and sisters/with,
Black beamers and/white picket fences/
And perfect identities.

If Black and White were simple and right.
But, one is always wrong.
If black and white were: Just/Right…
And, then the eyes open/because utopia is only a dream.

Afro Chick in a Spring Love Mist

These braids going back all twisted and tangled,
Like rows of corn in a field of charcoal.
Long braids of an afro chick…
Is this what he's digging?
I believe it's me, he is digging,
Cause each braid lock I take loose,
I see him watching hungrily.
He wants to loose my brassiere.
Yes! I'm about to be freed, with each gasp,
As his hands slide down my back, unclasp the clasp,
I'm a sister queen in a spring love mist,
Each cotton strand must be carefully picked,
By his strong brown fingers, warm thick,
The touching liberation of an afro chick.

Angel Wings of Prayer (Feathers out to Sea)

If prayers are carried to God's ears,
By His angels to heaven, on their wings,
Like songs of peaceful doves that sing,
Yet, hopeless cries endlessly ring.

And prayers of knowledge cross God's mind.
Why does wisdom so often elude mankind?
Or prayers of kindness pierce God's heart,
Then why do we tear each other apart:
Still prayers of love touch God's graceful soul,
We throw it away, like miners toss, fool's gold.

Because some prayers are carried on angel's wings,
Without binding faith to God's righteousness,
Without hope, LOVE, and true sincerity,
They slip off during flight, like feathers in the breeze
Falling, back to earth, or floating out to sea.

Beautifully Black (Important in February)

My beautiful black
Goes way past my skin, my sin
Way past white children held on my bosom
And lashes carved in my back from master's whip
Way past Deep South, where slavery ends
My beautiful black is far reaching within
Politically correct; Afro-American
Deep down in cotton, I'm hidden
I made the cotton Gin
Where would the world be?
If it saw beyond my skin
A visionary of freedom
If I wasn't label as good, evil
A descendant of Adam, not Cain
A creator of hope or medical discovery
From the start, a closer of open hearts, surgery
My beautifully black is deeper than kissable full lips
The disco jam, afro bell bottom, shaking hips
I wish my beautiful black was not so secondary
Was not so ordinary, everyday appreciated
And not just understood in February.

Beholding Beauty in Simple Things

If beauty is in the eye of the beholder,
Then I choose to behold the beauty,
In the lucent sunrise…
The vulnerable skin between my thighs.
The profound passion in your eyes.
The sweat trickling from your brow,
As you grind against despair to save our lives.
The kiss you place on my baby's forehead…
When I'm nervous, the way you rub my leg.
When you are furious with me, how you still,
Let me kiss your neck.

The lingerie hanging in the closet,
Waiting for infatuated sex.
Rainfall cascading, anointing my head,
Washing away expired regrets.

You whispering… "what's next?"

What's next?

The soft petals of a flower picked by hands.
Loves me… Loves me not…
Thus my heart perpetually sings,
For beauty is often found in simple things.

Birth of a Mommy

A girl of about eleven years in age is sitting on a beach by the calm ocean, with a woman.
Both are staring at the aquamarine sea as it foams into white peaks, when it reaches shore and then softens again into cooling blue.

The girl turns her head away from the rippling water and stares up at the woman and
asks:

"What is the difference between a mother and a mommy?"

Not even turning her head, the woman replies:

"A mother gives life to a mommy and a mommy gives life to a mother."

The girl looks at the woman, with a confused look in her eyes
 and says:

"What?" "But, that means they are the same."

The woman looks down at the girl and smiles, then replies: "Yes, sweetheart, they are. But, a mother gives life and a mommy gives life like the distance of the ocean."

The woman turns her head towards the water, again.

The girl says, "Oh." Then she too, turns her head and looks back out at the sea.

There was silence, except for seagulls in the distance. They both had reached an understanding.

Blue Skies into Rain

We loved each other from the very start.
But we couldn't see past broken hearts.
We knew our love was meant to be,
But you and I didn't believe.

If we could have taken a simple chance.
Our true love would never have ended.
Yeah, it's time we let each other go,
Because our hearts shouldn't hurt anymore.

Yeah, I don't know what happened to you.
I don't know what happened to me.
We turned our blue skies into rain,
And now our hearts can't take more pain.

I don't know what happened to you.
I don't know what happened to me.
You turned my blue skies into rain,
And, now my whole world's gone insane.

Real love's so hard to find.
It's not always on your mind.
If it's not embedded in your soul.
It will be impossible to hold.

We had all the makings of true love.
Something sweet, sent from above.
But, then our love had lack of faith.
And, turn our blue skies into rain.

Yeah , we let fear stand in our way.
So, there's nothing left to say.
We let our fears stand in the way.
And turned our blue skies into rain.

Boxed In

You want me to live inside this box.
Because, they say it's "So new and hot!"

You want me to wear that dress.
Because, it shows my breasts, best.

You want me to pierce "WHAT!"
So, we can get our vibe up.

You want me to paint my face,
Like the cover of a magazine.

Well, I got news for you!

Here's what I want, too.

I need you to leave my space,
So, I can get a natural break,
From this artificial zoo,
Because, you don't have a clue, OF WHO

I AM…

Capital Puppets

Cash Puppet rack, rack it
So you can get your stacks
And squash the ghetto
Indigenous, step back

Pole puppet dance, dance
So you can get your chance
And rock that trick check
In the south of France

Book puppet, street smarts lost
Now, you can infiltrate corporation
And count your stock loss
Impress a "real" boss

Art puppet feed them the hook
So, get in the kitchen
And grind poetic rhyme
Shake off haters, shook!

Now, handle this truth…

Chocolate Fervor (Chocolate Fever)

I'm about to call emergency
Because, I got something going on feverishly
The absorption of this velvety Chocolate
Is giving me the sweetest kind of headache
This morning…

See he "warned" me not to take him in.
I did.
Chocolate drops like this does wonders for the skin.
Life savers.
He said: "I'm just letting you know."

I said: "Stop talking. Give me the flow."

Then, and then… and then…

The sorrel! Cascaded down like cocoa milk,
Hot on the epidermis.
Tell me what kind of mahogany is this.
Making me heat, flush, I'm on febrile.
The intensity is undeniable…

Whew! Someone call the paramedics, please.

Wait! He said: "You need to try some morning coffee, or hazel nut tea."
"I think it's the cure for your ferment disease."

Please!

Please, please… please… too much mocha, lava consumes me.

Soothes me… completely.

I think,
I'll cool off with some caramel sauce dipped in fudge ice-cream.

Confessions of a Hypocrite

I laugh at my pain because it is customary.
I cry out with laughter because it is necessary.
I cringe at my beauty because it is superficial.
I judge all my friends because I am perfection.
I wallow in sin because I'm only human.
I point my finger with false pretence.
And drown my sorrows in alcohol on weekends.
I have fabulous wardrobes because they say so.
But, deep down inside I'm rotten to the core.
I provide for my family everything financially.
But, rob them of true love, purposefully.

I am condescending,
And uplifting.
I am rejection,
And all accepting.
I have sympathy with no traces of empathy.
I preach for peace,
And secretly desire war.
Man, I seemed to have fool,
But, God knows truly my soul.

Dirty Talk (Talking Dirty)

Why! How dare you speak that way?
So, despicable and wicked!

Like stripping the dignity of a little babe.
Clothed in merciless, naked shame
Caused by grown probing hands,
Having invaded innocence!
Like frightened lambs awaiting scraping claws,
In dire suspense!
Is it too intense?
To dirty? To convince the fellow man,
That dirty talk "isn't cheap."
The cost, it seems insurmountable, vain.
Yet, it releases malevolence, dark secrets.
Like evil skeletons caught in the Light
Dancing, laughing celebrating in the night.

Trash talk penetrates the hardened mind and
Soul of the clueless and the aware skeptic…
Like a vile bee driving into the very core of
A celibate, naïve Rose…

Pinching pollen only generates poison honey.
Counterfeit sweets must not be eaten by children.
But, by unashamed, ravishing earthly souls.

Here, not to create Love and Life:
But, sadly, only to eradicate it.

This, Friday (Easy)

Tonight, let's forget the club, scene
Started doing that, when I was sixteen
Yeah, I know, it's Friday night
We'll take it easy, alright

Yes, baby, you and me
Just "chillin," Harmony
We can talk, Politics,
Or things that make you sick,
Or watch a horror flick.

Maybe even, sip some booze
If that's the thing for you
I'll have some hot tea
Just stay at home with me

Then, I can rub your chest
While kissing on your neck
And, you can make me sweat
Okay, you know the rest

Next Friday, we will see,
Hit that club, on….
"What's the street?"
Tonight, just stay home
And take it Easy.

Explain This (Strange Hold)

Explain why you act surprise,
Like I don't see love, in your eyes.
Explain why after you stole a wish,
You make believe, I don't exist.

You can't explain this,
To your friends.
When your watching me,
through your lenses.
And, you can't explain this,
To you crew,
How you feel at night when I'm,
Touching you.

Explain why, when the love we make,
It's so hard for us to separate,
Explain when "I say, I'm in love with you."
You pretend so much, that you never knew.

Bet you can't explain this.
How it feels…
How it feels,
So good, when our lips meet.
Bet you can't explain at all,
This strange hold,..
This strange hold,
That won't let you go, your heart.

First Date (COLD)

Can I see you again, sometimes?
MAYBE.

Can you come up for a drink?
IT'S LATE, BABY.

Can I call you, soon?
YEAH. THAT'S COOL!

Can we hang as friends?
THAT'S A PLAN.

GIRL, LET ME GIVE YOU A HUG.
Shrug.

YEAH, THAT WAS REAL NICE!
Goodnight.

First Date (WARM)

Can you see me, again?
NO.

Can you come in for a drink?
DON'T THINK SO.
BESIDES, I DON'T DRINK.
Not even wine?
DUDE, STOP WASTING TIME.

Can you call me up?
NEVER.

Can you be my friend?
MAKE OTHER PLANS.

Can you give me a kiss goodnight?
ALRIGHT!

For a Black Cause (Bettin on Black)

Don't use the natural color of my skin
For your reverberating causes of sin
Don't take my black in vain
To ease false corruption and pain
Don't use my black for a "good" cause
Then imprison me with bias laws
Don't use my black against prosperity and wealth
And, then leave me the one deepest in debt
Take that black power poster down
Cause I'm just a "nigga" with my pants hangin down
Why are you bettin on black to preach equality
Cause Lord knows, you don't give respect to me
You keep using my black for empty causes
Not looking inside to see where my heart is
My black is my birthright, my culture, my Zen,
It does not reflect my soul and love within.
My black is my birthright, my culture, my Zen.
Only true love can reveal what I have to give.

Groove Rainbows (Rainbows are Fairytales)

I believe in you/do you believe in me?
Rainbows are fairytales/that drift across the sky/
Why are the colors all the same/never getting out line?

You and I are both the same/blending colors/out of range.
So, baby just believe in me/and, this world we can change.

I believe in you/do you believe in me?
Shake me to pieces, baby/back to reality/
Mix up the colors, baby/back to reality/
Mix up the colors, baby/set true colors free.

Cause rainbows are fairytales/and I only dream in grey/
Cause rainbows are fairytales/ and I only dream in grey.

Groove me your colors baby/and I'll wash your pain away.
A grey rainbow needs true love to brighten up the days.
A grey rainbow needs real love to wash the pain away.

I need to be in Love with a Taurus (Soul Mate)

Inspired by Love

I was in love with a Taurus…
He captured the essence of me.
With him there was only happiness,
On a whole new level,
But he was in love with another…

I was in lust with a Scorpio…
He played with my emotions,
By, stroking my body to ecstasy.
He had me yearning, constantly,
I could not see,
He was bamboozling me…

I was bonded to an Aries. physically, mentally, and
Legally,
But, not spiritually.
Yet, he would not let go of me,
Until he broke the very core of my being.
And, then he did not need or want,
Whom I had come to be.

I need to be in love with a Taurus…
He knows me.
He accepts my triumphs and my fallacies.
My passion for life burns and overflows with him.
He renews my soul…
I need to be in love with a Taurus.

I'm Not in Love with Your Swag (In Love Behind the Scenes)

I'm not in love with your amount money,
I'm not in love with your tailored clothes,
These are all things I've seen in life, many times before.

I'm not in love with your swagger
Even though, your presence stops me cold
It has my heart suspended, suppressing love,
Like an unfound diamond in the rough.

I'm not impressed by your guest list,
Or people that you "ball out" with,
Or the cars we roll together in, when we take a ride…
Just hold me close at night and say: Baby we're alright.

I just want to close my eyes in peace and have sweet dreams.
Because, I'm in love with you behind the scenes.

Other girls may love you for the superficial things,
The shine, the limelight, the glamour and all of what it seems to bring.
But, even if you lost it all and never gained those things, again,
My heart would still only be in love with you,
Cause right now I can't even speak…

You've swept me off my feet…
And, right now I can't even breathe.

Your love for me has taken my air away,
And I can't even breathe.
Because, I'm in love with you, behind the scenes.

I Don't Need No Mistletoe (Jazzy Mistletoe)

I don't need no hung high mistletoe
To feel his love, I do adore

Forget about those jingling bells
They can't remind me of his swinging smell

His smooches taste like peppermint kiss
Lingers on my mouth, he doesn't miss

Old spiked eggnog won't get me drunk
I'm swaying from his powerful hugs

I'll forgo that smooth, jazzy mistletoe
Don't need it when he kisses me, so

Well, goodbye carolers, just leave me be
He's got me singing by the Christmas tree.

Superficial exteriors can block true interiors, stay true to who you are…. Janett Jones

So many friendships and love connections are missed because of lack of communication… I don't know, but I've heard it somewhere before

Just Take Me

Take me as I am.
Take me with my stellar dress and "Jimmy hoo's,"
With my t-shirt and jeans,
And my no- name brand shoes.

Take me as I am.
Take me with my luxury car,
My rental, my handle bars
My top notch watch,
Or one bought hocked.

Take me as I am,
With my crazy head of hair,
Or none that is there.
Take me as I am.
Don't knock the rocks,
Or the holes in my socks.
Don't disrespect what you see,
Because when this stuff is gone.
It's just you and me.

Take me as I am.
IF, YOU LOVE ME.

Love Letter to a Fiancé

You want me to save your life.
You want me to be your spouse.
How can I make this sacrifice?
Or feel your love on sleepless nights.

Your soul I haven't seen in light...
Do you want me to make it right?
Then prove with trust, you're worth my time.
And, bring true love with all your might.

Although my wish is to hold you locked,
To stay with you until our dying hearts.
Thus, we must stand and will have to fight,
And, band against the looming dark.

Love Song of Jacinta

My eyes are closed and I am unable to see you without me

And it will take until the earth is blinded

Like glass grains of sand reflecting unyielding light into my eyes

For me to let go of your heart.

It will take the sea drowning the sun on the horizon

Before I can release the grip you have on my soul.

My eyes will remain closed…

Keeping tears from falling

Like grass forever impeded by trees from spring dew.

Before I can ever fall out of love with you.

Make Simple Love (That's Why)

It would be easy just to say,
I love you.
And, never tell you why.
Because it's to hard to stop,
Loving you.
and, easier to say goodbye.

So, just please make simple love,
And never ask me why.
Because, simple love needs no words,
Requires no explanation,
Yet, robs the heart and soul, blind.

That's why in an instant
I turn away when you look
Me in the eyes.
That's why in an instant,
I whisper yes, so you can,
Turn back around and try.
Cause if I give you simple love,
For true love, you will not strive.

Midnight Stand

The motel was freezing.
I OPENED my eyes…
He was next to me breathing,
With his mouth ajar.
Midnight air was more pleasing.
I nudged his muscled shoulder.
"What?' He grumbled.
Then he opened his eyes,
And looked at my strange face,
You look different without makeup…
I wanted to say, SHUT UP!
But, he said it was a good thing.
Then, he went back to sleeping,
And, I back to thinking; thinking,
Wait until he sees my hair in the morning.
Yet, his snoring was quite annoying,
So, I grabbed my things,
Dressed too hurriedly,
Opened the motel door,
To go face more cold.

On a Summer's Day (Maybe on a Friday)

On a summer's day,
Maybe on a Friday
We will reminisce of days gone by.
How much joy we had,
How you made me laugh,
And cried, and impossibly mad.
When you said I was too fat,
Then I said you were too thin,
Yet, the birds whispered in the wind,
"You two are perfect for each other."
So, I clung to you on Friday and forever.

One summer's day,
When we are both old, gray,
We will be eternally young.
We will be infinitely passionate,
Remembering our struggles and triumphs.
And, we will remember making our children,
By moonlight on beaches of white sand,
While sand fleas nibbled at my skin.
And how you mocked me as I scratched and complained,
While you rubbed me down with soothing cream.
Then, you said you would never leave me,
But I knew it wasn't true, yet I believed.

On a summer's night,
Possibly on a Friday.
I will look into your eyes,
And say: "I love you."
You will not reply the same.
You will not utter a sound.
You will just touch my face.

Peanut Butter Speaks (Peanut Butter is Talking)

She speaks:
And she says,
Why do you want me to kiss you?
Your mouth is cursed, unclean
You heart is really angry and not for me
You talk bad to me
You roll up your sleeves
And poke fun at things
You don't understand
You look in the mirror
And you are my gift
God's gift to a woman
Your rampages make me shake
You screw me hurriedly
Plus…
Plus… you have peanut butter in your teeth.

His sticky mouth speaks:
He says,
Then, why do you love me?

She sighs:
Then says,
We have sorted history…
Plus, God only knows this mystery.

Photographing Beauty

A photograph can only chill beauty for
A depthless moment
Snapped, facile elegance often transudes
Falsely into memory from a picture
Causing one to view love simply
Merely the hazel eyes or baby blues
Twinkling pearly whites
Full lips by candlelight
Flowing dark hair

Oh, a vibrant air!
This beauty…
Illustrating externally.

Yet, somehow, as I depict
A Love so true
My discernment always forms
A montage of you.

Please Believe Me (When I Say)

Please believe me when I say
I remember you, I remember you
Like yesterday
Please tell me you love me, dear
Whisper a gentle breeze, gentle breeze
In my ear.

Please believe me when I say
I remember your touch,
I remember your smile,
I remember your hugs,
Like it was yesterday.

Please believe me when I say,
Grab hold of my hand,
And we can fly, fly away,
To distant lands.
If you'd just hold on to me,
And, try to remember what we had.

Remember my heart,
Remember my soul,
Remember my kiss.
No other love is like this,
No other love is like this…
No other love… take my breath.

Poppa Holiday (Holiday Poppa)

Poppa said, "Baby I'll be home this holiday."
Said he'd be bringing his Love this way,
So, I warmed up my body with the fireplace.
And, I heated up my heart for his snowy embrace

Poppa said he'd always know my lovely name,
He wasn't like the others; oh no, not the same.
He said, "I'm much better than that Mr. Claus."
Don't worry; you're dealing with the right boss.

So, I went to the airport, a rainy Saturday.
Hoping for a blue box, Tiffany's!
Waiting for my sweetheart patiently…
My true love, my man, Poppa Holiday.

At five past twelve, I knew everything changed.
My crazy, mad love was put to a crying shame.
My happy holiday was dead, rearranged.
His soul "missed" the devotion plane.

My mind was lost, my heart to blame,
Because, Holiday Poppa never came.

Powerful Hero (One Time Country Girl)

One time…
I was a country girl of about age nineteen
Waiting for a powerful hero to come rescue me.

Two times…
I was in fairytale love, blind and couldn't see
With shining knights of steel, riding in the wind.
But, real life brought me one with the most foremost love
He set my naïve heart on fire and then he set my body free

One time…
When I was a country girl with big city dreams
A gentle caller knocked down my door
And pulled me into a world of diamond rings
Who knew the most prevailing love
Would knock me off my dirt road feet
Then turn right around, slap my face
Bringing me to my praying knees

Two times…
He gave commanding love when he looked into my eyes
But, back then I didn't have the strength
Too fight off his consuming lies

One time…
My love was so very patient and far too innocent
Didn't know love could be so bitter and at the same time be so sweet.
Because, I was just a little girl in a small mundane world
With fantasies of love, I was told in Cinder… tales

Two times…
Now, that I'm a country girl with a burning city heart
I finally realize I needed to love myself, right from the very start
And, One time…
Is plenty of time for a simple girl to complicate some things
So, super man, come straighten it out and take some love from me.

Power Running Things

Power runs through the soul
Like an electric bolt
Of lightening
With energy
To run the world
Or ruin it.
With the potency
To save lives
Or take them to demise.
Power running things…
Halting dreams…
Causing screams…
And silencing.
Silencing…

Silent power
Is not without strength
It is not weak or meek…
But, a smooth supportive
Pulse
Without fuss.

Serendipity

In the foregone year of ninety-three,
Meeting you was not serendipity,
Our love is not merely lucky,
It is not a fantasy dreamt...

I did not stumble upon you
In a case of serendipity.

What I see in you is not from a casual glance,
What I feel from you is not an accident,
My love, I will not bestow another being,
Our souls are meshed together in destiny.

What you want to know is fated entirely in romance,
Love clings to your heart, like dew in vineyards of France
Stop suppressing what you feel and ultimately require,
For true love is never incidental karma.

Stop suppressing, the inevitable that's you and me,
For true love is never serendipity.

Spicy Fight

When I have a spicy fight
With my sweetheart late at night
We do it right, non-violent.
With each stroke his beating heart screams
Against my chest, against my breasts.
Uncontrollable, smoldering.
Never instigating, just coaxing
Coaxing is in motion,
Like waves of the ocean.
Only laying hands where I need
Softly biting, when I plead
Spicy fights are instant
They don't last that long,
But are infinitely needed,
To keep our love strong.

Sunday Daze

Woke up this morning
In a Sunday Daze
Looked into Baby's sad eyes
And this is what I said:
Look at how the trees dance
Swaying in the breeze
This is God's signal
That we are alive and breathe
Listen to the birds sing
Hear them how they praise
See, they already know that
Everyday is God's given Day
See, we are only alive
Because of His Mercy and Grace
And, breathing fresh air
Means happiness
In every State
So, put on your 'holy" shoes
Even when it's not so "cool"
And even, when Man makes you cry
Stand strong right by his side
And say:

I'm living my life everyday
In a content, blessed way
And I'm feeling just fine
In my lovely Sunday Daze.

Surviving Jasmine (For Loss of a Child)

Surviving something so small
Seems too enormous
Giving birth is so harmless
Unless breathing is not normal
Five toes, fingers not moving
People shouting
Doubting, holding breath
But breathing
Large- numbered wall clock loud, ticking
Rushing MDs, nurses, not hesitating
Resuscitating…
Resuscitating in vain
Remembering a tiny heartbeat
Ears hear wrong, eyes strain
Seeing a lifeless doll, no pain
Doesn't have a name
They seem happy to claim…

Her…

Must get a name in time
It's February.
A lost valentine.
A present from God…

Now, he needs her back…
Young angels don't last long…
On Earth!

"What do you want to name her?"
Nurse X asks, impatiently asks
She seems too cheerful, happy?
Having survived an angel, "Jasmine."

The Year for Release of Minor Things

Minor things race across our minds
We feel we have wasted time
We fail to seize the moment
Letting our tears fuel anxiety
Of the coming New Year
Will I have enough money?
Will I get my bills paid?
Will I have a place to stay?
We live fearful and in duress
Yet, God somehow makes a way…

If only we would realize
That worry devours
Causing peaceful hearts to cower,
Humanity to stress and sour.

Please remember you're here
Remember that lives were lost this year
Yet, you and I are still here:
Breathing, crying, cheering.
Not fearing…
Not fretting about things not done
About a future, that hasn't come.
We must say no more…

I say no more:

This is the year I released minor things.
Brought inhibited love into fruition.
Focused on my God given vision…
And, started on my purposeful mission.
I will use what I've been given…

Unthankful

I'd be unthankful if I didn't know your name.
I'd be unthankful if you didn't grab my hand,
Pull me to the floor and ask me to dance…
Without your sturdy body blending with me

I'd be unthankful if my children weren't born
Or not hearing the voices of my dearest loved ones
What about living in a land without choices?
Not being able to observe the beauty of horses.
I would be unthankful if the color blue did not exist
To dye the ocean, where I can feel the water on my feet
I would be unthankful if soldiers had no reprieve
If scientists stop trying to cure, untreatable diseases

I would be unthankful if time stopped infinitely,
Because infinite is never enough for you and me.

Rebel Seventeen at Hamburger King (Young Love Rebel)

Big cities and college life consumed her love.
She wasn't particularly careful
Walking through downtown streets in a tight, cotton black dress
With a slit to reveal… her soft soul?
She made it on a sewing machine
Her mother bought her when she was fifteen:
Her mother forbade her to wear the dress to school.
Whatever!
She disobeyed because she was proud of her creation
And wanted to be sexy and free
After all, she was an intelligent freshman
In sophomore and junior Biology
She could make wise decisions
She could do her own thing
She wasn't a little girl; she was grown.
Grown: living with her momma.
Not like the homeless bum
Who asked her for money every day she passed by.
He made her want to laugh and cry.
Because he was grown and could not make ends meet.
Now, he was living on the streets begging pitifully
Not to eat, only to buy alcoholic drinks.
Her judging heart was better than his
After all she was in school for an MD degree
She was determined not to catch his disease
But cure his body and mentality:

She said follow me to Hamburger King
To get something to eat
He could have killed her for that twenty.
The girl behind the greasy counter laughed with her eyes.
Her eyes spoke; they said fool with a Fool.

Rebel seventeen didn't care,
She bought the smelly dude a burger meal and drink
And wondered what her mom and dad would think.

Thank you for reading my poetry, my blue flames. It's been a pleasure to share with you something deep from my mind, heart and soul. Please look for my third volume of Odes for the Soul… Poetry That Heals, coming soon December 2012.

Remember to love infinitely… J.R. Jones

Love comes in many forms; hurt isn't one of them.

www.ingramcontent.com/pod-product-compliance
Lightning Source LLC
Chambersburg PA
CBHW041308110426
42743CB00037B/32